The King Who Understood Animals

The King Who Understood Animals

A Jataka Tale

Illustrated by
Magdalena Duran

Dharma Publishing

Jataka Tales Series

First published 2002

Second edition 2009, revised and augmented with guidance for parents and teachers.
Cover design by Kando Dorsey.

Printed on acid-free paper

Printed in the USA by Dharma Press, 35788 Hauser Bridge Rd., Cazadero, California 95421.

9   8   7   6   5   4   3   2   1

Library of Congress Control Number: 2009938989

ISBN 978-089800-520-2

www.dharmapublishing.com

Dedicated to children everywhere

Once upon a time in the land of India, a ruler of the nagas, powerful beings who dwell under the sea, left his watery realm and entered the world of men. Taking the shape of a snake, he traveled far from his home, crossing rivers and forests in search of adventure.

Near the ancient city of Benares, two village boys noticed the snake. Shouting, "A snake! A snake!" the boys ran toward the naga, throwing clods of dirt and striking him with sticks.

Their cries were heard by Senaka, king of Benares, who was on his way to visit his garden. Seeing the snake's distress, the king told his attendants, "Do not let them hurt that harmless snake! Go quickly, and make them stop." As soon as the two boys stopped harassing the snake, it slipped into the bushes and disappeared.

The naga did not forget King Senaka's kindness. After he had returned to his undersea realm, he filled a basket with jewels from his treasure house and then went back to offer it to the king.

The naga said, "Because of you, I am still alive," and gave King Senaka the basket with precious stones. So grateful was the naga that he gave the king an even more exquisite gift: a secret spell that would allow him to understand the language of animals.

"My friend," the naga said, "remember that this is a powerful spell. Do not tell it to anyone, or you will die immediately." The king accepted the spell, and from that time on he could understand what all the animals around him were saying.

One day King Senaka and his queen were eating cakes and honey. A handful of crumbs, a drop of honey and a bit of molasses fell on the ground. An ant who was foraging close by called out to his friends, saying, "The king's honey-jar is broken! His molasses-cart and cake-wagon have fallen over! Hurry up so we can feast on honey and molasses and cake!"

The ant's excitement over such tiny bits of cake and honey made the king laugh. The queen was curious and looked around, but could not see anything funny. Twice more the king – hearing the love songs of flies and the chatter of other insects – broke into laughter. Now the queen thought the king was making fun of her, and she became upset. "My lord," she said, "please tell me: why are you laughing?"

At first the king tried to distract the queen by telling a joke. But she only became more anxious and insisted that he tell her the truth. Finally he gave in to her pleas.

"I was given a magic spell that opened my ears to the language of animals," said the king. "I hear them say very amusing things. But I cannot tell you more. If I reveal the spell to anyone, I will die on the spot."

The queen was very beautiful and the king loved her dearly. But she was young and used to getting her way because of her good looks. Thinking, "This is a very special gift. I must have it for myself," she teased and coaxed the king until he promised to tell her the magic words.

No sooner had King Senaka uttered this promise than he realized what he had done. Just to please his queen for a few moments, he had rashly made a promise that would bring his death. He became distraught, wondering what would become of his people when he was no longer around to protect them. But the king had given the queen his word, and the word of a king must not be broken.

Wishing to see his favorite garden one last time before he died, King Senaka stepped into his horse-drawn chariot and drove out of the palace gates.

At that very moment, Shakra, king of the gods, looked down from his heavenly realm and saw what was about to happen to the king.

To show the king that he was making a big mistake, Shakra and one of his maidens took the form of goats and appeared on the king's path. Leaping and bounding about in front of the chariot, the goats annoyed the king's horse.

Snorting and stamping his feet,
the horse called out to the goats:
    "'Goats are stupid,' the wise man says.
    These words are surely true.
    You foolish goats disturb my king
    and cause me trouble too.
    Don't you care what you do?"

The goat replied,
"Look at you, poor old horse!
There you stand, tied up with ropes,
looking worried and out of sorts.
When you are loosed you don't run free;
isn't that a foolish way to be?
Yet the king you carry here
is even more stupid than
you, I hear."

The horse apologized saying,
 "What you say is true of me,
 and that is plain for all to see.
 But my king, a foolish man?
 Please explain that – if you can!"

With a toss of his head the goat replied:
 "The king has a great treasure
 that he would give to his wife.
 He knows she cares mainly for pleasure,
 and still he entrusts her with his life."

Intrigued, the king encouraged the goat to go on.

"O king, every living being
knows that life is far more
precious than gold.
What right have you your
life to give,
When your people depend
upon you to live?"

The king asked, "King of goats, who are you? Why are you here?"

The goat replied, "I am Shakra, and I have come to save you from death, out of compassion for you and your people."

"O ruler of the heavens," said the king, "I know you speak the truth. Yet I cannot break my word. Tell me, what can I do?"

The goat Shakra replied,
"A thoughtless promise made today
may cause great suffering tomorrow.
When this is true, it rests on you
to prevent this coming sorrow.

You proved your worth to the naga
before he gave you the spell.
Your wife must follow custom
and prove her worth as well."

Then the two goats changed back into their godly forms and disappeared. Pondering Shakra's words, the king drove on to his garden and asked that the queen be brought to him.

When the queen arrived, the king told her that those who wanted the spell had to prove they were worth it.

"How does one do this?" asked the queen.

"You will receive a hundred blows of a bamboo stick and must bear them without making a sound. Is having the spell worth that much pain?"

The queen was so eager that, without thinking, she said yes. But when she saw the man with the bamboo stick approaching she became scared and cried, "No! I was wrong! I do not need the spell!" Looking at the woman for whom he had nearly died, the king spoke sadly, "You were willing to see me die and leave our people without royal guidance and protection. Now you must do your best to prove that you are worthy to be their queen." Sobbing with regret, the queen bowed her head and promised to redeem herself.

From that time on, King Senaka was well aware of the danger of selfishness and greed. Respecting the power of his own words, the king never again made foolish promises.

And the queen? Coming to realize how much she and her country had nearly lost, she changed her ways and devoted the rest of her life to helping others.

Under the naga's protection, the king and queen
lived to a very old age. Seeing clearly what was
true and good, they took care of everyone in the
kingdom, and ruled wisely and well.

The Jataka Tales nurture in readers young and old an appreciation for values shared by all the world's great traditions. Read aloud, performed and studied for centuries, they communicate universal values such as kindness, forgiveness, compassion, humility, courage, honesty and patience. You can bring these stories alive through the suggestions on these pages. Actively engaging with the stories creates a bridge to the children in your life and opens a dialogue about what brings joy, stability and caring.

The King Who Understood Animals

When he saves a naga's life, King Senaka is given a secret charm that empowers him to understand the speech of animals. Revealing the charm, however, will bring about the king's death. King Senaka listens to his queen's plea for the charm, and gives in. When he realizes the destructive selfishness of her greed, it is too late. The king is saved from his folly by a wise goat's advice.

Key Values
Integrity
Kindness to animals
Leadership

Bringing the story to life

Engage the children by saying, "In this story a king receives the power to understand animals – but if the king shares the spell, he will die. What do you think happens when his queen persuades him to reveal the spell? Let's read the story to find out."

- Why does King Senaka help the snake? Who is the snake really?
- What is wonderful about the king's secret power, and what is dangerous about it?
- How does the queen find out about the king's ability to understand animals?
- How important do you think the king is to the queen?
- Why does the king tell the queen the secret? Would you have done the same thing?
- Why does Shakra help King Senaka? How are animals important in saving his life?
- What prevents the queen from learning the secret of the charm? What would you be willing to do for a precious secret?

Discussion topics and questions can be modified depending on the child's age.